*B*OB'S BOOK IS AN *essential excursion into the world of narrative theology in six easy steps. The power of stories flowing back and forth in a healthy economy of exchange can literally change the world. When there is blockage of this flow, problems abound. Our work at Drew University's doctor of ministry program is literally based on this type of research, and I would not hesitate to recommend this book to my students as they research how to improve their church contexts. In that vein, I offer this pound cake recipe with the hope that those who read the opening and closing narratives might actually enjoy the food that brought the two characters together and facilitated their story sharing.*

— Dr. Daniel H. Kroger
Adjunct Professor, Drew University
Madison, New Jersey

Pound cake owes its name to the traditional ingredients—one pound each of flour, butter, sugar, and eggs—which remain essentially the same today.

1 lb. butter (1 box salted)
1 lb. sugar (2⅔ c.)
1 lb. eggs (≈8xl)
1 lb. flour (4c.)

Ingredients should be room temp.
Beat and beat and beat the butter.
Add sugar and beat and beat again.
Add eggs and beat gently until the egg yolks are broken into small pieces.
Add flour and fold or mix until ingredients are just mixed smooth—don't over beat.

Put into a well greased Bundt pan and bake at 325° for 1 hr. 10 min. (depends on the oven). Check at one hour.

My Pastor, My Money, and Why We're Not Talking

Tom,
Keep the conversation going

Rob
12-13-12

My Pastor, My Money, and Why We're Not Talking

Bridging the Gap Between Pastors and Those with Wealth

Robert Moon

WITH A FOREWORD BY JOHN KILLINGER

THE INTERMUNDIA PRESS

2012

Robert is a public speaker as well as an ordained minister and is frequently a guest minister or interim pastor. He holds a BA in sociology, an MDiv, a DMin, and an MBA. His residence and wealth management firm are located in Northern Virginia.

My Pastor, My Money, and Why We're Not Talking: Bridging the Gap Between Pastors and Those with Wealth
by
Robert Moon

THE INTERMUNDIA PRESS, LLC
Warrenton, Virginia

ISBN 978-1-887730-27-3

To order additional copies of this book, please contact

THE INTERMUNDIA PRESS
www.intermundiapress.weebly.com

DEDICATION

To my beloved wife of 13 years, Benjalyn (Benji) Jane Johnston Byers Moon, 1946–2012, who never felt uncomfortable with prosperity because her spirituality encompassed both the necessary provisions and the abundant blessings from God in bad times and good.

Contents

Acknowledgements

I MUST BEGIN BY EXPRESSING deep gratitude to the client couple who first introduced my business partner and me to the gap that is frequently present between the clergy and those with extraordinary blessings. It is their frankness in expressing their journey and their permission to use their story anonymously that released us to pursue a serious dialogue among clergy and other financial professionals.

I am grateful for the clergy persons and accountants who responded openly and honestly to our probing questions about their experiences (or non-experiences) with the affluent regarding spirituality and wealth. This initial research was a joint effort with my close friend and business partner, Mark Cooke, who as majority owner and president of our company saw the wisdom in doing this research and providing this tool that both clergy and the laity might use to open dialogue and ultimately ministry opportunities.

Likewise, I appreciate the other members of our company—Elizabeth Clarke, Dave Morton, and Cyndi Cooke—all of whom encouraged this production and allowed me time for reflection and composition.

A very valuable source of encouragement has come from my good friend, John Killinger, who was so kind to offer feedback and write the foreword. When it comes to the purpose of this book, he gets it.

The big hurdle of bringing ideas and concepts to print was easily overcome with the expert guidance of Eric Killinger and his publication skills through The Intermundia Press.

Finally, I am grateful for the support of my adult kids—Jay, Josh, Amber, Sam, and Summer—and my sister Gwen, who encouraged me to pick up the pen and move forward with ministry through the written word and living anew each day.

Foreword

A CLERGY FRIEND WHO WAS pastor of a large Baptist church in Louisville, Kentucky, showed up at a seminar where I was speaking. I was happy to see him. After the seminar, we had a Coke together and he told me how low he was feeling.

"What's the matter?" I asked. "Your wife kick you out?"

"Funny," he said, listlessly. "No, it was something I did."

"Care to talk about it?" I asked.

He mused for a moment, then opened up. "It was last Sunday," he said. "We had a good worship service. My sermon went well. We gave the invitation."

"And nobody came?" I prompted. Baptist invitations always fall flat if nobody responds.

He smiled. "Oh, somebody came. Three somebodies, in fact. A middle-aged banker and his wife, and a ten-year-old boy who accepted Christ in his Sunday school class earlier that morning."

"So?" I waited.

"So I made a big fuss over the banker and his wife. I heard they had visited us a couple of times, and I was excited about their joining our congregation because I knew the guy had been a heavy donor and a real spark plug in the congregation they were coming from. I practically had him tagged to be our next pledge-drive leader."

"And. . . ?" I waited for the punch line.

"I fumbled the ball," he said, shrugging. I made a big deal over the banker and his wife, and in my excitement about their joining I almost overlooked little Jimmy Carruthers, the ten-year-old who had come to Christ that morning."

"Did anybody say anything?"

"No. Everybody else seemed as pleased as I was. But I realized on the way home from church that I had failed that little boy. I had called his name and said we were glad to have him accepting Christ, but that was all—and I know I must have spent at least five minutes talking about the banker and his wife."

"And now you're tortured by this?"

"Darned right I am. I really goofed."

I've often thought about my friend's confession. I'm proud of him, that what he did actually bothered him. I also understand why he did it. Most pastors don't ever have a lot of money. So when somebody with money and power joins the church, they tend to fall all over themselves welcoming them. Churches exist to promote spirituality, but they don't run very long on spirituality alone. They need money. Lots of money. The bigger the church, the more money.

I have to confess that my problem has been the opposite of my friend's. I've probably always felt too little regard for the well-to-do members of my churches. In most of my congregations, I've had a lot of wealthy constituents—prominent doctors and attorneys, financiers, presidents of insurance companies, owners of factories and construction companies, and people who simply inherited fortunes.

But I never felt that these folks deserved more of my time

than ordinary parishioners. The truth is that I probably paid more attention to street people and folks on welfare than I did to them. Somehow I was always haunted by Jesus's saying about the rich man and the eye of a needle.

How I wish my friend and I and all the other ministers I know could have had this book of Bob Moon's to read as we were entering our ministries! What a spectacular difference it might have made to us and the churches we pastored!

Imagine a parish where pastors and their more prosperous members actually discuss the privileges and perils of wealth—where the pastors don't take it for granted that the wealthy can take care of themselves—where stewardship is viewed as a lot more than contributions to the church's upkeep—where members from both ends of the financial spectrum can dialogue regularly about their needs and the needs of others and how they can satisfy the demands of Christ on their lives.

What a completely different atmosphere there would be in churches where this kind of thing happened!

How responsible it would be!

And how *Christian*!

In light of this book of Bob's, it occurs to me that most of our seminaries have failed us by not including any courses in Christian finance in their curricula. They simply assume that pastors will know how to deal with wealthier members and feel personally comfortable among them. To be totally honest, I doubt if there are many professors with the kind of training and experience that would qualify them to teach such a course in the seminaries.

Bob has given me a new appreciation for ministers I know who successfully pastor their wealthy members. I realize now that I shouldn't regard them as somehow unspiritual or subchristian.

On the contrary, they probably provide a kind of pastoral leadership to the well-to-do in their congregations that pastors before them failed to give. It isn't any wonder that many of their more prosperous members adore and even idolize them.

In my novel *The Zacchaeus Solution*, I imagine a church where people meet the needs of the poor in their community by talking about those needs and actually banding together to make important things happen. Almost by accident, the minister in the story, Rev. Jack Myers, becomes closely involved with wealthier members of his congregation and inspires them to start a revolution of giving and caring for the less fortunate around them.

But Bob Moon has taken that formula a step further. He asks for a more conscious effort on the part of every minister to provide the sort of pastoral care for well-to-do church members that will almost certainly lead to the kind of revolution that I've described in my book. He doesn't leave it to accident. He poses situations in which pastors consciously initiate discussions with their wealthier members about the Christian use of wealth, for the sake of the prosperous members themselves as well as for the sake of the poorer members of their community.

This book could well revolutionize Christianity in America today, and, after that, in the world at large.

For this to happen, all we need is for churches in which the kinds of conversations Bob Moon envisions begin to take place and Christians of all social strata and financial backgrounds actually discuss together the role of economics in their lives.

When it happens—when it *really* happens—we'll be a heck of a lot closer to what Jesus called "the kingdom of God."

JOHN KILLINGER

Preface

IN THE TYPICAL DIALOGUES between a clergyperson and a parishioner, one might easily overhear conversations that explore a wide range of subjects. The conversation could be a sharing of blessings—I just got a raise. We are getting married. We are pregnant. Jimmy is coming home. Susan graduates this week.

What can be overheard can also include the stresses that might be present in a person's life—My child is in harm's way serving our country in the war. We have been to the doctor and we are awaiting lab results. My brother died. Robert lost his job. Our son is into drugs. Our daughter is pregnant.

There are many subjects that are freely discussed and shared between pastor and parishioner. Except . . . except the subject of wealth. One's wealth is rarely discussed. This absence of discussion is not because there is a lack of wealth. There is ample evidence that wealth exists in parishes. There is also ample evidence that its presence is avoided in discussion. This book deals frankly with this void, in other words, why wealth is rarely discussed in church or between pastor and church members. Its intent is to suggest ways that this void can be bridged through the beginning of dialogue between pastors and their affluent members.

Why take on the matter of wealth discussion between clergyperson and parishioner? It is the belief of this author that one of the major dynamics always at work in the Christian church at large and in the individual lives of believers is the ever present tension between the practice of faith and the day-to-day economics that pervade every aspect of our lives. Tremendous spiritual growth and maturity are being missed among the laity and pastor alike when wealth conversations are off limits.

This book is *not* about prosperity religion. Rather, it seeks to find ways for pastors and parishioners to discover a comfort zone of dialogue that freely engages spirituality in the presence of wealth. There are many voices that address spirituality in the presence of poverty. There are more voices—even more needed—that call attention to the needs of the poorest in our world as a spiritual matter. But there are fewer dialogues that address the specific stresses where wealth is present. It is this author's belief that our global community would be greatly benefited if more honest spiritual dialogue occurred among those with wealth.

The following chapters suggest six obstacles that might be blocking such a spiritual and fruitful dialogue between clergy and laity regarding wealth. Three of these obstacles have their origin with the clergy. The other three obstacles reside with the laity. Each chapter addresses an obstacle by identifying it and acknowledging its presence, and then it explores what the clergy and the laity can do to overcome that barrier.

In several places the author has inserted a typical scenario in which the issues of pastoral care, spirituality, and wealth intersect in the presence of pastor and parishioner. The reader is cautioned at this point not to debate the particulars of the illustrations. It is not important whether the details or rationale match your experience or values. What is important is that one sees in these vignettes the opportunities in other occasions, your occasions in which you and your pastor can be receptive to the spiritual issue that is present.

The intent is to open dialogue between the person of wealth and the pastor so that each can better understand the opportunities for growth in faith and spirituality.

It is suggested that either the pastor or the lay person take the initiative to present a copy of this book to the other with an invitation to meet and discuss each other's reactions to what is proposed. This dialogue could begin as a group discussion. However, the specifics surrounding one's wealth can be quite sensitive and deserve the utmost privacy. Therefore, the deeper conversation would be best served in quiet one-on-one conversations between the pastor and the individual. The ultimate objective is to begin the dialogue.

Let's get started.

PART I

Introduction: Sudden Wealth

MARGARET, RECENTLY WIDOWED, RECEIVES Pastor Tom at her back door off the driveway, ushers him back into her kitchen and to a seat at the table which a few months ago was loaded with cakes, pies, casseroles, and gallon jugs of sweet tea. That sudden feast was the expected response of a community to the shocking news that Richard, her husband of 30 years, had died of a heart attack while on his annual salmon fishing trip with their boys. Today, the table is covered by a well-worn red plaid vinyl cloth material and a single place mat. Margaret offers Tom a cup of coffee, remembering that, like Richard, Tom likes his coffee strong and black.

Previously, Pastor Tom dropped by frequently and sat at this table to move the Kinsley family through the many facets of grief. Their kids had crowded around this extended table to discuss the details of the funeral service. He remembers the cramped conditions where the family and friends pressed their way through the narrow passages of chairs, and ice chests alongside stacks of Tupperware-packaged cakes and pies to feed the crowd that milled about the formal living room and spilled out into the den below, the porch, and onto the lawn under the big oak trees out front.

Tom planned to come by this week or the next to check on Margaret's progress, but she had called and asked for him to come by today. After taking a bite of the fresh pound cake set before him, Tom begins the conversation by asking how the kids and grandkids are adjusting, now that the routine of school is well underway. Margaret chats freely about each of the three grandkids, and how the oldest, Trey—now 16 and able to drive on his own—drops by frequently to check on her and mow her lawn. She then intentionally directs the conversation by saying, "Pastor Tom, yesterday I had a visitor from the Academy Life Insurance agent, a Mr. Knowles, and he presented me with this," as she slides a check-sized piece of paper across the red plaid toward her preacher. "I need to talk about this," she says nervously, and adds, "Never imagined that I would be faced with this much money."

Tom flips over the check and sees it is a check from the Academy Life Insurance and Annuity Company of Nebraska made payable to Margaret Leslie Kinsley, Beneficiary for Richard Lewis Kinsley, in the amount of $75,000.00. Tom is quickly relieved that Richard took some good action long ago to help his beloved wife survive his absence. Tom's eyes linger over the check and he realizes before he speaks that he misread the check. It is not for $75,000.00. He is not familiar with this many zeros. It is for $750,000.00. "Holy Jesus," he thinks in the back of his clerical mind, this is three-quarters of a million dollars.

Before he can think of what to say, Margaret pushes an opened envelope to him and says. "This also came in the mail this morning." Tom glances up at Margaret and sees her blue eyes are welling with tears and pleading for help and explanation. He pulls open the envelope and opens a letter from Henderson Electronic,

Inc., Steubenville, Ohio. He reads the letter silently, getting the message from Richard's employer: . . . *we are deeply grieved at the loss of our beloved employee Richard and will forever remember his work ethic as a model for other employees.* It is hand signed by the president of Henderson Electronic, Inc. Sliding from the folds of the letter is another check, this time from Madison Employee Benefits and Insurance, Richardsville, Kentucky, made payable to Mrs. M. L. Kinsley.

The amount payable is more carefully studied by Tom this time and his lips read, "Two hundred fifty thousand dollars." He notices the memo line reads, Employee Death Benefit for Richard L. Lewis. Tom does some quick, simple math and realizes he is now sitting at the table of a millionaire, a sudden and shocked millionaire, a millionaire wrapped in grief with no experience with large finances. He pauses for a moment to take in what has just been delivered to his pastoral care scope of service. His eyes again meet Margaret's, alerting him that he is venturing into financial territory that is beyond his salary, but smack in the middle of what it means to deliver pastoral care.

He takes a bite of pound cake and another sip of coffee, buying time to think of how he will respond. Nothing he can recall in his seminary classes in pastoral care or church administration comes readily to mind to offer him a launch into what he will say next as soon as the coffee clears his throat. He ponders for a second if he should take another bite of pound cake.

This scenario should be happening frequently. It should not be unfamiliar territory to the typical pastor who has conducted a significant number of funerals for parishioners and walked with the survivors in a journey called grief. Unless the pastor's parish is embedded in the midst of an impoverished community, the probability of a survivor being a beneficiary to some life policy is at least 50 percent, and even higher if the deceased was employed at the time of the death. The amounts might vary greatly, from 5,000 to five million, but the impact upon the survivors can be similar.

The direction the conversation will take between Pastor Tom and Margaret will determine if the relationship between this clergy person and this now affluent parishioner will be helpful or harmful. Furthermore, what happens in this kitchen conversation could have repercussions for years to come as word spreads among family members, fellow parishioners, and community members about how Pastor Tom served Ms. Margaret in her surprise moment of sudden affluence . . . and vulnerability.

MISTAKE № 1:

STEWARDSHIP AS THE PASTOR'S MAGNETIC NORTH

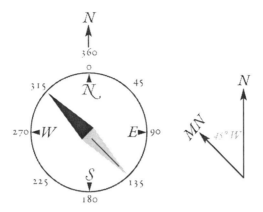

MY NUMEROUS CONVERSATIONS WITH pastors about a scenario as described in the introduction reveal that a large majority of pastors' initial take on the discussion of money with their parishioners frequently centers on stewardship. By stewardship, and in this discussion, I mean the layperson's typical understanding of stewardship when coming from a pastor, church, or religious setting. That typical understanding of stewardship is the support of the mission or objective of the church through the donation of money.

Indeed, there will be arguments from my clergy colleagues and well trained laity that the concept of stewardship encompasses more than finances, and I agree. But the reality is that when a scenario of what has been offered in the introduction is presented for discussion, it is the clergy in most cases who too frequently have the involuntary reaction of thinking that stewardship means the financial support of the church.

A case in point: when we conducted our original research on the matter of pastors having conversations with their parishioners about the parishioners' wealth, we continually encountered the automatic presumption that our subject matter was how the pastor can get more financial support for the church from those who are affluent. When we promoted workshops with the specific title "Pastoral Care in the Context of Wealth," the clarification of the topic to be discussed focused on the delivery of pastoral care to those who have pastoral care needs related to their wealth. We discovered that the invitation to a seminar to address this specific need was being pre-empted with an automatic assumption that the seminar was about stewardship. We heard clergy persons invite lay leadership and other pastors to come hear what Bob and Mark had to say about stewardship—with the overtones that the subject to be discussed was the support of the church from the resources of the rich, rather than how to provide pastoral care to those who happened to be affluent.

This observation supports my theory: Parishioners are reluctant to address the challenges they are encountering that are peculiar to the possession of wealth because they have been conditioned over the years to believe that the pastor's response will be one that has already been heard. The affluent have come to expect hearing the pastor say something like this:

> *Praise the Lord! We rejoice in your good fortune. Margaret, when you asked how you might address some of your issues now that you have wealth, of course we need to begin with giving at least a tithe, if not more, of your financial blessings to the church. And there just happens to be a missions program, a capital campaign project, or an operating budget shortfall where your blessings, and of course your generosity, could be the answer we have been praying for. We*

have been pleading with God to help us financially meet the challenge to fulfill what we think is our calling. We have been trusting God that if we are doing what we are called to do, that the resource will come. We have been faithful to pursue that calling, and it appears that you are the answer to fill that gap. Praise God! Isn't God always faithful? And isn't God always full of wonderful surprises?

This is an example in which the clergyperson's preoccupation with the financial stresses within the operations of the church as a business gets sucked into the automatic responses that stewardship in the context of wealth is always the answer, and again, stewardship is tracked specifically to the needs of the religious institution. I call this *institutional abuse of stewardship*, because it places the importance of the survival of the institution ahead of the pastoral care needs of the parishioner; in other words, the church's financial situation has priority over the needs of your family or the community at large.

What is at stake when institutional abuse of stewardship bulldozes over the concerns that are present with affluence? Let's examine one of the major risks pastors take in allowing stewardship to be their magnetic north when it comes to the finances of their affluent parishioners. It is the risk of predetermined expectations. If the parishioner constantly hears in communication from the pulpit, the teaching lectern, the newsletter, and the campaign letters that the church comes first when it comes to finances, then the parishioner is conditioned to believe that the pastor's fiduciary responsibility to the church will always override the pastor's pastoral care for the total welfare and spiritual health of the parishioner. The affluent can expect that the pastor will not hear the agony about the fear of poverty in one's old age, the wrangling of family members in the transition of wealth, the protection of obligations that one has to the community at large and to other businesses. How can my pastor hear my concerns when it appears that his or her only concern is how to meet the budget or wrap up this capital campaign?

WHAT CLERGYPERSONS CAN DO TO CORRECT THE MISTAKE OF PRESUMPTIVE STEWARDSHIP

I suggest that the place to begin is to embrace stewardship from a global perspective. Stewardship is the management and accountability of resources. Those resources could belong to another person or entity, in other words, a company, another individual, an institution, a community. Those resources which require stewardship could belong to the person and to no other entity.

Regardless of who owns them or where those resources originated, the concept of stewardship is not limited to money, but rather encompasses all resources. For example, the resource could be property, time, energy, attention, focus, even love.

The key operative verbs in the definition of stewardship are management and accountability, making the best decision among many alternatives that will enhance the impact of the resources to their maximum use. A major component of management and accountability is determining priorities and being guided by a disciplined approach rather than whimsical response.

When it comes to the perception of affluence, the application of stewardship might well begin with the priority of taking care of one's self so that one does not become a financial burden later in life. Daily encounters and discussions with persons of affluence reveal to me that one of the major concerns of the affluent is to protect their resources while they are alive so that those resources will avoid any financial burden upon those they love. In plain English,

> I don't want to be a burden on my children. I want to take care of myself for as long as possible. I want to be independent. I don't want my health or physical needs in my final chapters of life to drain away my kids' future. Mr. Financial Advisor, can you help me do that? Pastor Tommy, can you understand what that goal means to me? And do either of you have any idea how much of my resources on hand that will take to accomplish my goal? The last thing I want to do is have had all this provided to me, for me to let it get away, and then in my old age, be a ward of the state or require that my adult child go bankrupt trying to take care of me. I would rather die than to be that irresponsible with my resources. I need some help.

The pastoral care challenge in this context is to understand that stewardship is global. In global stewardship there is both management and accountability of resources from one generation to another. It is the taking care of one's self so that one is not a burden on others.

We have found in our discussions with the affluent, or even mildly affluent, that if they can have some reasonable assurance that their resources can be expected to take care of their needs for the remainder of their lives, they are then more willing to be generous. This is global stewardship in its purest application.

WHAT MORE PASTORS CAN DO TO AVOID THE MISTAKE OF INSTITUTIONAL STEWARDSHIP ABUSE

Pastors can begin this transition by acknowledging their own vulnerabilities and missteps. How refreshing might it be to the affluent to hear the pastor confess: "I have been making stewardship and support of the mission of the church the automatic answer to all things concerning wealth." The confession might go on to provide explanation of how that vein of thought began. It probably did not begin in seminary, as most graduates seeking their first parish have deep passions about truly helping people in need and providing spiritual resources to meet life's greatest challenges.

After a few years in the real world of church leadership, the pressure to keep the church alive financially can seem to demand a narrow financial presentation of stewardship. Additionally, most seminary graduates, if not entering the ministry as a second career following serious business experiences and significant amounts of money, have no experience in understanding or conversing about financial concerns of any magnitude. Clergypersons can confess how they have been thinking and where they want to go.

Finally, the clergy can ask for help. It can be as simple as the clergyperson privately asking one who is affluent, "What can you teach me about your needs? What are the special burdens you carry? What am I saying or doing that turns you away before we can begin a dialogue?"

HOW THE AFFLUENT LAITY CAN CORRECT THE ALIGNMENT OF STEWARDSHIP AS A GLOBAL MATTER THAT GOES BEYOND THE WALLS OF THE CHURCH

I would suggest a parishioner's frankness, expressed in kindness and concern, can provide great help to the clergyperson who truly wants to be effective in ministry to all of his or her constituents, not just the poor.

Here are my thoughts. First, when you see the predominance of stewardship as being about the church and donor rather than a global acknowledgement of wider scope of concerns, the affluent member can gently point this out. It is probably more effective over coffee or tea in a private setting.

Second, when you have an issue you want to discuss that involves your resources, you might want to clarify what you are seeking. For example, you might frankly say,

> *I do not want the typical knee-jerk solution I have heard all my life, namely, give it to the church, or be sure to tithe. Rather, what I am looking for is someone who is willing to understand all of the dynamics at stake with my resources and can offer me spiritual insight into those dynamics.*

Finally, it is fair to be asked to be heard in the context of your concern, not the context of the concern of the church. If you cannot get a hearing, then you might need to take your concern to a spiritual advisor who will listen without a handout.

GLOBAL STEWARDSHIP

MISTAKE № 2:

ADDRESSING POVERTY IN WAYS THAT ALIENATE THE WEALTHY

THE BLUES AND COUNTRY music playlists have at least one common theme that is present in many of their songs: poverty. It seems that there is an art to expressing experienced poverty in such a manner that it connects with listeners and turns them into fans who will purchase tickets to concerts and buy the latest recordings. It seems that the greater you can describe your own poverty or some other person's poverty, the more money you can make as an artist.

I have witnessed the same among ministers. Sometimes ministers tell stories that identify them with an existence among the poor when in fact they are far wealthier than they let on. During his ministry, my dad called it "poor mouthing"; in other words, setting the stage with the audience about just how poor they were at some point in their past (to supposedly identify with the poor in the audience, or to show their own rags-to-riches story), or how poor they are now (in order to validate their plea for support through contributions to their cause). My dad was guilty of the latter. I frequently heard his illustration about just how poor our family was when he was in the early stages of establishing the inner-city mission for the homeless and derelicts. The story went something like this:

> Things were so bad at the time. I needed good dress clothes but couldn't afford them. So, I prayed fervently for the prosperity of my personal pastor for him to have the resources to buy a new suit. Whenever he would get a new suit, he would give me his old one, and I would make it work for me.

Of course he always got a good laugh, and so did his pastor. Whatever the objective of this illustration, it seemed to work effectively. It made him appear to understand what it means to be poor and therefore made him popular with those who also knew what it meant to be poor, either in their past or presently.

Some pastors seek to identify with the poorest in the community by presenting poverty as the norm, acceptable, understood. It is a way to appear in sync with the poor, but it can come at a great cost of alienating those in the audience who are affluent. How can this pastor who brags about how poor he was or is and implies that there is some sense of purity, honesty, and wholesome earthiness to being poor ever comprehend what my challenges are with the presence of wealth in my life? He brags about eating chicken and getting from one meal to next, and I never think about my next meal in terms of hunger. When it comes to a meal, I think in terms of presentation, how it will look to my guests, and the most fitting place to have it, whether in my home, the country club, or one of our favorite five-star restaurants.

Other examples of how ministers portray poverty as more righteous and wealth as less godly include describing characters in biblical stories who happen to be wealthy with derogatory implications and making the rich the butt of jokes. It might connect with a few who feel the rich have done them in, and it might get a good laugh; but it spurns the opportunity for the affluent to sense any inclusion in the faith community.

Another way that the clergy alienate the affluent person who might be a serious seeker of spiritual truths is setting up an image that most, if not all, persons of wealth somehow obtained their wealthy status by ripping off the poor and vulnerable, cheating on their taxes, or conducting business unethically or illegally. Such an overstatement is very painful to hear if you happen to be wealthy because you worked hard, honestly, and ethically, or you happened to be very fortunate in an inheritance or sale of property for which someone was willing to pay handsomely.

Another turnoff to the affluent person is promoting the idea that wealth is something bad, capable of corrupting the soul, and should be given away as quickly as possible. We call this the "Franciscan Cloud," a takeoff on the historical St. Francis of Assisi, who as a young man gave away all his wealth from his family and family business as his interpretation of salvation and devoted his entire life as a priest taking care of the poorest in his country. Akin to this is the emphasis of the rich man who came to Jesus as a seeker of eternal life, and when told by Jesus to sell off what he had, give to the poor, and follow him, the man walked away very sad because he had great possessions (Matt 19:16–22).

What is at stake when poverty is presented as more pure and righteous and wealth is projected as evil, even something shameful? It sets forth an unmistakable anti-wealth prejudice that people of wealth are somehow less human, even less humane, than those without affluence. Possession of wealth is perceived by the poor and the affluent as a sin, in other words, one should not have wealth, that it is contradictory or hypocritical to claim oneself as a follower of Jesus and be wealthy at the same time.

If one were a member of a racial or ethnic group, it would be highly unlikely that this person would seek out a therapist known for being a racist if the counseling needed to be about racism. The same would logically apply that a person of affluence would not likely seek pastoral care guidance regarding one's wealth if the pastor is always telegraphing negative signals of suspicion and anger toward the wealthy, even when it is disguised as overblown praise for the poor.

WHAT CLERGY CAN DO TO CORRECT THIS MISTAKE

I believe the most fruitful approach to correcting this mistake is to confess to automatic mischaracterization of the wealthy and stereotyping of the affluent. The pastor can begin by sharing in a confessional mode, either through sermons or teachings, his or her early conditioning in social and spiritual development that cast a cloud of suspicion or jealousy on those who had more than others. The clergyperson can then move openly to ask for help to learn what is at stake, what is felt, what is experienced, how this wealth occurred, what is one's most valued possession (which could have nothing to do with money or wealth).

WHAT THE AFFLUENT CAN DO TO CORRECT THIS MISTAKE

First you can ask for a private audience with the pastor, in which you share your story that shows who you are, not what you possess. Then it would be very helpful to ask the pastor to listen, without judgment or quick remedy of the solution, to your struggles and fears that may be present within your wealth that may not be known. In truth, the fear of poverty (or the return of poverty) can be devastating to those who have experienced unusual access to the best in life and living conditions.

MISTAKE № 3:

UNDERVALUING CONFIDENTIALITY

THERE IS AN UNDERLYING assumption about confidentiality, namely, anything of a personal nature that is discussed with one's pastor or priest is considered privileged information. Sometimes one or both parties might underscore that what is being shared is a confessional and neither the pastor or priest nor the parishioner will share this information without explicit permission of the other.

There is, however, more to confidentiality than what is addressed in a confessional booth, a counseling session, or a hospital room. One of the most neglected areas for the practice of confidentiality is in the arena of finances and wealth. Let me share with you a story that I gained second hand from a pastor who followed a previous pastor who had mistakenly undervalued the church member's need for confidentiality. I have changed the details and the names to protect identities.

Roy has been pastor of the Easy Creek Community Church for two years. Strategic plans have been carefully developed with congregational input and approval. One component of that strategic plan is the capital campaign, which is currently underway.

Roy is not comfortable making calls on parishioners for the purpose of obtaining financial support, but the pressure has been put on him to discover why a certain individual is not responding to the current campaign. His name is Stephen, and he is known to be privately wealthy in land holdings and mining rights. His presentation in frayed overalls, faded plaid shirts, and scruffy beard cannot camouflage what the local people know. The public tax records reveal his land holdings, and most of the realtors in town know that Stephen was the quiet seller of many large pieces of property during the past two decades that amounted to several million dollars on land free of any debt.

For several decades, Stephen had quietly given sizeable contributions to the youth fund, the restoration of the pipe organ, and the renovation of the church library. But in the past five years he has not provided any gifts except his monthly offerings, which are dependable and much needed to keep the church going.

In the current capital campaign Stephen has been non-responsive to phone calls, letters, and attempted visits by the campaign committee solicitor. The professional fundraising consultant that the church hired for guiding the congregation through the campaign has finally convinced Roy that it is now his responsibility as pastor to explore Stephen's resistance after so many years of strong support. Reluctantly, Roy has arranged a meeting with Stephen in the privacy of his home. After conversations about the weather, the crops, the family, and the dog, Roy eventually directs the topic to the reason for his visit with Stephen.

— Stephen, you probably suspect one of the reasons I am here today. It is about Easy Creek's current capital campaign. I have been your pastor for only two years, but I understand that in times past you could always be counted on to help out in a sizeable way. But currently we are hearing nothing from you, and I am here today to learn more about your past giving and what we might discuss about your support for our current campaign. Would you be willing to share your thoughts with me?

— Well of course, Pastor Roy. I appreciate your visit. Yes, I have been very quiet this time around about all the hullaballoo on the capital campaign. First, let me assure you that I am not against this strategy. It makes perfect sense to me. Two million dollars is a lot to ask from this little church and community, and that might be a big challenge, but I understand the reasoning.

— Stephen, I am glad to hear your support of this venture. That means a lot to me and to our church. So I am curious why we have not received any response from you regarding a personal pledge or gift. Could you share with me your feeling in that regard?

A long pause follows, as Roy watches Stephen ponder his reply, expecting the words that come from lips to be either a rage or carefully expressed. He is thankful for the latter.

— Pastor Roy, first, my non-action has nothing to do with you. I like you. I like your sermons. And I like the way you have cared about my well-being.

What dampened my enthusiasm for making sizeable gifts to the church happened a few years before you arrived at Easy Creek. Indeed, I would be grateful to share it with you. In the last campaign for building the annex to the church a serious mistake was made, and I am still feeling the repercussions. As you know, I pledged a half million dollars. What you might not know is that that pledge was to be strictly confidential, anonymous. I emphasized that to the campaign chairman and the pastor at the time I made the commitment. Somehow, some way, it was spilled in a campaign committee meeting that they had raised $100,000 and that Stephen was good for a half million.

That was true, but the problem was the violation of confidentiality.

— Stephen, I am very sorry to hear that. Can you tell me more?

— That pledge was contingent on the sale of a piece of property that was under negotiation and close to a final contract and closing date. The unfortunate announcement in that committee meeting back then triggered a leak of information and an assumption that my offering price was somehow matched to my pledged donation, about a $100,000 gap. Based on that assumption, the buyer, who is local and on that committee, tried to whittle me down from $600,000 to $500,000. It soured the negotiation and the deal did not go through. Nevertheless, I honored the pledge because I could. I have been blessed. But this irresponsible action by a member of that committee became almost a curse. It was just the beginning of a string of problems that remain to this day.

You see, when I honored my pledge, that donation came out of my estate rather than from the intended sale of the property. My son, who is very protective of me, and of course protective of his future inheritance, found out about this gift and became very upset. I knew he might; that's why I needed my gift to be confidential and anonymous. He left Easy Creek several years ago to attend a more contemporary congregation with that loud music and a preacher who uses overhead slides all the time. He thinks any large gift to Easy Creek is a waste of the family's resources. So, my generosity to Easy Creek has become something that has brought nothing but tension between me and my family. I'm not sure I want to, or can, be as generous as I once was. And I am still upset about my confidentiality and anonymity being violated.

After their conversation concluded and Roy made his way back to his office, he felt sick. A man's trust had been violated by the church, and an opportunity for the church and the donor to be blessed had been severely tarnished. The damage was done, severe. He pondered if there would be any chance of recovery during his tenure as Stephen's pastor.

There are other ways confidentiality is violated, or appears to be violated.

Mary listens from her usual seat on the third pew from the back as Pastor Tim attempts to interpret Paul's second letter to the Corinthians:

> [Regarding your giving,] there should not be relief for others and pressure on you, but it is a question of a fair balance between your present abundance and their need, so that their abundance may be for your need, in order that there might be a fair balance (8:13–14, NRSV).

The pastor explains,

> Let me give you an example of how this works. I know a lady who took care of her sick husband during a long period that drained all their resources and they barely got by. There were those in the congregation who recognized that crisis and responded with gifts of food, money, and in some cases with the doctor, medical care at no charge. Her husband passed, and a few months later she received a six-figure benefit from her late husband's life insurance policy. Her first response was to go to her pastor and make a donation of one tenth of that unexpected benefit. Today she continues to be blessed, because others were willing to bless her in her time of need.

Mary is suddenly frozen in her seat. That's my story. He didn't mention me by name, but everyone close to me . . . my friends . . . all know about Bill's long illness and the need to sell the house. And several of these people, including Dr. Williams across the aisle, did support us in our financial struggles. And yes, I did give a tithe of that insurance settlement. But why has he just told the world? Everyone knows this person is me and they now think I have a very healthy bank account again.

Meanwhile, Jack is setting on the opposite side of the sanctuary, and he is feeling a sense of pressure from the pulpit, as though this scripture and this interpretation were aimed at him. Yes, Sally's final days drained our account, and yes I did receive a death benefit larger than I expected a few months ago. And I did share this blessing with Pastor Tim. I feel he is digging at me from the pulpit to give him or the church their fair share. I swear I'll never talk about my finances with him again.

What is at stake when confidentiality is violated or anonymity is not respected?

Many people regard their financial matters as extremely private and personal. Many times even their family members do not have any idea of their net worth, what is owned, how it is titled, who is owed, and what will go to the heirs. Persons who believe their confidentiality has been violated will freeze and become unwilling to take the risk of divulging what they might tell their pastor. I don't want my confession to be another illustration from the pulpit, a newsletter, or a teaching moment. It will be a long day in Hades before I share anything about my money.

As illustrated in the story of Roy the pastor and Stephen the generous member, sources of one's wealth can be placed at risk when information about their wealth are implied through donations. A donor contributing $100,000 to a building campaign might not want her heirs to know of this allocation away from the estate.

Additionally, there is the risk of wealth; for example, one's net worth on paper today could be poverty realized tomorrow, and vice versa. Pledges highlight that risk, where generosity is genuine in good times when the pledge is made and can be easily fulfilled, but a twist in a contract, a lawsuit, a collapsed investment, can render a pledge incapable of being honored and embarrassing to the one making the pledge.

Finally, there is the real risk of security. Persons known to be affluent are at higher risk of danger to family or other persons simply because of the perception that they have wealth. Not having immediate access to liquid wealth does not deter the scam artist, the bleeding heart, or the thief under the influence of mind-altering drugs.

WHAT CLERGY CAN DO TO CORRECT THIS MISTAKE

First, I suggest that clergy only use actual stories if and when the individual has given explicit permission to share his or her story. Included in that permission is a clear understanding of the level of detail that would make the individual uncomfortable. Included in the delivery of the story is an acknowledgement that this is shared with the individual's explicit permission. This usually requires advanced planning. One should never use such stories off the cuff without thought of the impact and repercussions.

Second, fictional characters can be a safety net for delivering the point. Characters and storylines found in fiction, public biographies, journalistic reports, or movies can illustrate the point with clarity without violating anyone's confidentiality or anonymity. In truth, referencing a public story may have more impact because more people have a connection to the same story.

WHAT PARISHIONERS CAN DO TO CORRECT THE MISTAKE OF UNDERVALUING CONFIDENTIALITY AND ANONYMITY

It is always good to clarify, rather than assume, what you consider to be "under the cloak" of priestly confession and confidentiality. Underscore your value of confidentiality, and define what that means and the consequences of its violation to you and to others. Defining how the accountability for violation of confidentially would involve the offender is a stern reminder. Make it clearly understood. Finally, don't share with anyone whom you cannot trust.

PART II

IN THE FIRST HALF of this book, we identified three mistakes commonly made by pastors or the congregation that become barriers to offering good pastoral care to those who happen to be affluent. In this second half we will switch the attention to discuss the three major mistakes wealthy persons make that contribute to the absence of spiritual guidance and pastoral care, particularly around issues that have to do with wealth and money.

MISTAKE № 4:

SILO SPIRITUALITY

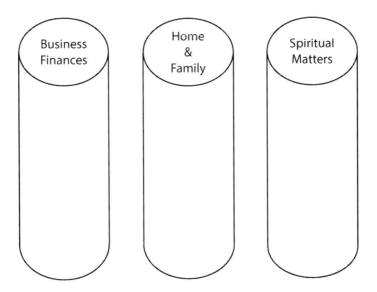

WHEN PERSONS PRIVATELY INSULATE their wealth and money from all considerations of spirituality, they are practicing what I would call "silo spirituality." A silo model for business is quite common. It can happen in a small or megabusiness. It occurs when various operations that are necessary to run a business are closed off from interacting with the other operations. For example, the purchasing, storage, and distribution of inventory—let's say the raw products for manufacturing—are managed by a person or group of persons expert in getting product into the business. Their expertise is needed to make the business profitable. They are really good at what they do, getting the best price for new materials and products. But they operate in another building or section and are completely set apart, with no communication between the other divisions of the business, in other words, sales, finance, marketing, quality control, manufacturing, distribution, etc. These other divisions operate with the same model, implementing their expertise in what they do, but unaware of what others are doing or how what they do affects others or the company's bottom line.

In business schools, this is recognized as a silo model, in other words, vertical self-contained cylinders standing side by side in the same field but not interacting with each other. As consumers we experience it frequently when we feel as though the left hand does not know what the right is doing—My bill is obviously out of touch with the sales department.

Silo operations or management is a frequent cause of business failure and even more so the larger the business. The silos just grow taller, sometimes even competing with each other to the detriment of the owners/shareholders, consumers, and employees. Supposedly, someone at the top is orchestrating all these stand-alone silos so that they produce a profit. Business schools have long understood that this can be a formula for disaster. The better model is the horizontal structure. Expertise is retained, but information is shared and integrated so that each section of the business is working toward the same goals. Sometimes it takes a bit more effort to keep all of the components communicating and learning from each other, but this effort reaps better rewards.

Affluent and wealthy parishioners are practicing silo spirituality when they believe that their affluence, their wealth, should have nothing to do with or be impacted by anything spiritual. In this model, the pastor's job is "to pray for me when I am sick, conduct a funeral when my family needs it, and stick to preaching on Sunday and operating the church during the week. Stay out of my business, stay out of my finances. You only need to be concerned about my giving to the church." Such thinking shortchanges the opportunity for faith and beliefs to positively impact our decisions about money, wealth, opportunity, and risks. If anything about our wealth or money keeps us awake at night, is a constant burden, or is tearing the family apart, then our faith, our spirituality, has a right to be present and accounted for in that context.

Roger, for example, has a big employment opportunity. Unsolicited, a nationally ranked headhunter specializing in finding executives in his field approached him several months ago to explore a new opportunity with another company five hundred miles away. It would mean a doubling of salary, greatly improved benefits, and an opportunity to become very wealthy with generous bonus stock options and a guaranteed pension plan. The question at stake: Do I take this offer? Is this what I really want to do, rather than what I really want to earn? This is a window of opportunity for pastoral care and the integration of faith, values, business, finance, and current and future wealth.

Quincy inherited her family's furniture business when her father passed away four years ago. She grew up in the business. She knows all the customers from 50 years back—who can pay cash for the top-quality sofa, who needs help with stretching out payments so they can get a children's modest bedroom set for their expanding family. She has her own series of television commercials, a fun outlet for her quirky down home humor.

Last month her biggest competitor expressed strong interest in buying her business. His offering price pleasantly surprised her. It is a figure higher than she has ever imagined— enough to carry her through a much needed retirement and to the end of her life, with a nice leftover for her grandkids.

In all her years at the church where she grew up and still attends, thinking about money was never present on her mind, except how to pay the bills, when she was in worship. She took counsel from her pastor when she went through a divorce and the death of a close friend but has never thought about seeking her pastor's guidance on what to do in the sale of her business. Her pastor, Kathy, furnished their home from her store, but Rev. Kathy knows nothing about the furniture business.

Willard has worked for his employer since high school. It has been nice to have a job through the tough times, getting married and establishing a home, raising three kids. Willard is starting to look down the road at the possibility of retirement in about 15 years. The company has never had a retirement plan. Fifteen years ago he was smart enough to start his own savings through an IRA for his wife and himself, but setting aside the maximum allowed has not produced enough to retire on, especially after that mess with the market in 2000 and 2008, respectively.

Three weeks ago his old high school buddy Rich approached him about starting a business. Rich had done his homework on this business idea. It indeed looks like a real moneymaker, with low overhead, low cost for materials, and a huge markup for an unbelievable profit margin. The only hesitation about accepting the offer is the type of business. Some might say that it is not illegal, but it is borderline ethical. It wouldn't be ripping off innocent people, but the line of business has always been preached against in his church denomination. And he has done a bit of the business on the side, privately. This business happens to be gambling—legal, but not something of which he thinks the pastor would approve. He is trying to convince himself that he has the right to do what he wants to do. "How I get my money is of no concern to the priest as long he gets his share in the offering."

These are typical gaps between one's faith journey and one's business and accumulation or distribution of wealth.

The foremost action is a personal awareness of our spirituality. Admitting that spirituality is present is the first step. Spirituality is embedded in our life more than we might realize or admit. From a beginning awareness as a child to our senior chapter, our life is a spiritual journey filled with decisions based on our ultimate and immediate values.

The next step is allowing ourselves to see how everything is indeed connected to our spiritual aliveness. This is not about doctrine or beliefs or religious formulas, but more about a sense that we are more than our possessions, relationships, and health. What we do with our wealth or affluence is guided by our spiritual values. If we are of the Christian faith, along our journey we discover at every intersection the validation of Jesus's teaching: *Where your treasure is, there your heart is also* (Matt 6:21, NRSV). Being aware of this begins bridging the gap between faith and our personal economics.

It is also okay to ask for help along this journey. That help can come in our private prayer life as well as the prayer of others for us during our decision making process. It is also okay to challenge what might seem to be the status quo regarding the welfare of your aging parents, your welfare as an aging parent, and your concern that your children not become wards of the state. These are all legitimate concerns along the journey of life and faith.

One of the practical ways you can begin to bridge the gap is to introduce your pastor to your work world. For example, invite him or her to attend a seminar you are presenting. Or invite him to visit your office, your place of employment, or the business you own. For a truck driver, it might be riding with you for a few hours and having a conversation around "your desk." For a person working in a very secure environment, it might be something as profound as meeting her for lunch at one the local eateries in your immediate work area. The point is to open his or her eyes to the environment that makes up most of your days and weeks.

WHAT CLERGYPERSONS CAN DO TO BRIDGE THIS PARTICULAR GAP, IN OTHER WORDS, THE ISOLATING OF WEALTH AND FINANCIAL ISSUES AWAY FROM SPIRITUAL REALITIES

First, I suggest opening oneself as a biblical interpreter to the economic realities and illustrations running throughout the scriptures and the history of the church. Some examples might include seeing for the first time the Old Testament patriarch Jacob at the river Jabbok as a lifelong entrepreneur who has become extremely wealthy but is running for his life. The book of Genesis portrays Joseph as the earliest economist and hedger with his radical use of commodities, in other words, grain. He bets on the famine. He is recognized as an economic genius, and the pharaoh is able to store more riches in his treasure through the sale of a commodity that is plentiful in Egypt but wiped out by famine in other countries.

The pastor also has the opportunity to confess if he or she has in the past chosen the ministry to avoid the headaches of business. Backing up that true confession with an act of repentance would be to begin to study the livelihood of your parishioners, show up at their workplaces to learn what they do to make a living, or go to lunch with them closest to their workplace and touch the base of their work environment. In other words, visit the marketplace. Be an Amos.

Finally, pastors can put down the biblical commentaries and stop restudying the same material that they have been pondering for years. You have spent many years of formal education focused on theology, doctrine, and pastoral care. You've got it! Commit to adding to your study the dynamics and concerns of your parishioners. Instead of—even better, along with—picking up another preaching journal, peruse the journals representing the professions in your parish in order to identify some of the challenges your working parishioners face. For example, in a community based on livestock, the journal might be on animal husbandry. Maybe you need to glance through journals on financing or health insurance or produce or defense contracting or military. Show up!

MISTAKE № 5:

AFFLUENT PERSONS IMAGINING CLERGY AS THE PREDATORS OF THEIR WEALTH

L ET'S BEGIN DISCUSSING THIS mistake with a bit of frankness. A predatory image of preachers and pastors has not come about in a vacuum. There are plenty of examples in which persons presenting themselves as ministers have literally ripped off the poor and the wealthy alike in religious schemes ranging from fraudulent investments to exhortations to "give me your money and God will bless you tenfold." In recent history these unscrupulous "clergymen"—many of them television evangelists—have been exposed, and some have spent well deserved time in prison. This chapter is less about this type of outrageous behavior in the name of the Lord, which in my opinion is the actual interpretation of using the Lord's name in vain. It is more about how the clergy are often perceived as always ready to receive the wealth of the affluent when soliciting resources for church operations, building programs, or mission projects.

In our discussions with many clergypersons and lay business people, there often is an open admission that the pastor is seen in an official capacity as the chief executive officer of the church. This perception is present whether it is the senior pastor of a multiple staff church, or a solo pastor of the congregation. There is an understood role of the pastor: he or she is responsible for the welfare of the church, making sure it does not go broke, that the lights stay on, and the doors are open to receive new members and convert many souls. The pastor is seen as the chief fundraiser. There may be an official fundraising committee, pledge committee, stewardship committee, or any of the many other names of committees that on the surface are in charge of raising support from the congregation or community. Yet these same official committees will often expect, sometimes demand, that the pastor support the fundraising efforts publicly, in newsletters, personal letters or mass mailings, and sermons from the pulpit.

I have heard committee members complain whenever they believe that they are receiving no support from the pastor because he never preaches about "stewardship and tithing." This is carried further when either the committee or the potential affluent donor expects the request for support to come directly from the CEO pastor.

In our research, many expressed their opinion that they thought it was the pastor's job as a chief executive of the church to make sure there is adequate revenue for the church operations and ministry. So for that very reason, they would not bring their issues regarding their affluence for pastoral care to their pastor because he or she might be wearing that CEO hat at the time, and the expected solution—or at least part of it—would be giving it to the church. That is one of the tasks of the preacher, so it's best to stay away from the preacher, particularly when the church is behind budget for the year or the pledge campaign goals have not been met. It's like saying, "I certainly wouldn't ask a hungry lion how to prepare this chuck roast for hamburgers!"

Akin to this view of seeing the pastor as the chief fundraising officer of the congregation is the message that is sometimes communicated subtly or shamelessly whenever the pastor conveys to his or her constituents an all for one, one for all perspective, such as, "Your wealth is God's blessing and God's spokesperson knows best how you should use it."

Here is an example of how that is telegraphed to members of a finance or stewardship committee or to an entire congregation:

> If all of us here, around this table, including myself, just gave a full tithe of OUR income, all of these challenges we have been facing here tonight would disappear. We would be figuring out how to do more with the blessings we would be receiving.

A statement like this exhibits a bit of judgment toward the listeners, assumes the pastor knows just how much they make, and demonstrates that the concerns of the church's finances far outweigh any needs that might be present in anyone's financial concerns for their family, their business, or employees.

So, what can the affluent do to correct this mistake, in other words, always assuming that pastors have their hands perpetually extended to collect as much as possible?

Perhaps the most powerful correction that can be made by those who are affluent would be to have frequent dialogues with the pastor, usually privately, in which you explore together the pastor's current struggle in that fundraising role. Begin dialoguing about how they feel about the yoke that is frequently placed on them. Is this role a blessing, a burden, a challenge, or the most blessed part of being a pastor? Exploring further how the operational funding or capital campaign is going can allow you to convey a concern for his or her welfare regarding these challenges.

The conversation could go on to include elaborating on the guidelines of any discussion about your concerns around your wealth.

> Pastor Beth, I know that you carry a heavy responsibility regarding the finances of this congregation. I appreciate that burden more than you might realize. You are responsible for more than yourself in these matters. I think it would be very helpful if you could understand that what I need to discuss with you is along those same lines.
>
> Many people, and some preachers in my past, probably think that I really have no money problems because of their perception of my wealth.
>
> The truth be told, Pastor Beth, I too carry a heavy burden connected with my wealth for some of the same reasons. I am responsible for more than myself in these matters.
>
> So, if you can, I would like for you to clearly lay aside your CEO hat and let me share with you what concerns me at this moment. Would you agree to help me in that way? I'll be glad to clarify when you seem to me to be putting on that CEO hat, and you can call me out when I start showing signs that I might be afraid you want some of my wealth for whatever reasons. Can we talk?

The clergy can take specific actions to help correct this predatory imagery. For example, when preaching or teaching about those scenes where there is an apparent contrast between wealth and poverty, take a step back, think about this from both the perspective of the impoverished as well as the affluent.

If you are impressed with the drastic actions that led St. Fran-

cis of Assisi to abandon all his wealth and possessions and take a
vow of poverty, consider also that for the rest of his life he relied
on others to take care of his needs, even if they were simple. The
idea of everyone taking a vow of poverty might not be the most
realistic solution to the disparity between the very poor and the
very wealthy.

The pastor can assist the laity in correcting this mistake by
openly discussing and acknowledging that the funding of the
church might not be the priority application of a person's resources. It can be a blessing to give, indeed, but not with a sense
of guilt or coercion.

MISTAKE № 6:

ASSUMING THE CLERGY ARE INCAPABLE
OF KNOWING YOUR CONCERNS
AND LEARNING HOW TO MEET YOUR
SPIRITUAL NEEDS SPECIFIC TO
YOUR AFFLUENCE

MARGARET AND JIM HAVE lived in their farmhouse all their married lives. Jim was born there 80 years ago. They inherited the farm from his father who passed away 30 years ago. Margaret raised their five children in this home, surrounded by barns and fields of corn, soybeans, stands of virgin hardwood timber, and a hundred head of grazing Black Angus cattle.

All the children grew up on that 1,500-acre farm and left for college thence graduate school, which were underwritten by the good planning and generosity of their parents. They are now scattered across the nation, in various high level jobs that have brought them huge success, McMansions in the suburbs, and their kids in top ranked (and expensive) colleges.

All of the siblings, that is, except one—John, who after college at A&M, returned to work the farm alongside his parents. He married his wife, Betty, a local girl, and they have remained on this farm, raising their children who are also off to college. They have shared their residence with mom and dad in the big old family home.

The other siblings are relieved that John and Betty are always nearby mom and dad, particularly since mom's stroke two years ago and dad's recent diagnosis with terminal cancer. The family is facing the reality that mom and dad will probably not live very long. Thoughts among them frequently but privately visit the question about what will happen to the farm. This question is relevant, because John and Betty are in their late fifties, and their children, who once were a big help running the farm, have chosen other careers outside of agriculture. John has made it clear that the farming of the land will probably not continue much longer. There is pressure from developers to turn the pastoral acreage into an upscale subdivision with 50–100-acre sites.

Thanksgiving is two weeks away. All the brothers and sisters and their families will once again attend this annual feast and homecoming, but this year there is an ominous tone developing as preparations for the gathering unfold. Dad is not expected to live beyond the winter, and mom's strength, endurance, and appetite are quickly fading. Though they each remain very alert and bright, they too know the closure of their journey is imminent. No one wants to take any action at this point regarding the future of the farm and land, but everyone knows radical changes are forthcoming.

Just a few years ago, an accountant shared this scenario with me as something that frequently is repeating across the large farming valley that runs through the state. He has witnessed how families have been torn apart with siblings not speaking to each other after the settlement of the estate of the parents. An accountant with a strong sense of values and faith, he wishes clergy could take a more active role in addressing situations like this. In fact, the cases he has witnessed as an accountant have similar parallels witnessed in the life of Jesus; in other words, brothers coming for advice on how to settle their father's estate, and so forth. In one case it might be the family farm; in other cases it might be the family business or a business owned by two partners, one of whom recently passed and is survived by his widow, who now wants to run the business her way even though she has very little working knowledge of what the business actually does day-to-day.

Our research has shown that the majority of persons who are affluent and who also consider themselves to hold deep spiritual values do not talk to their pastor or spiritual leader about the issues regarding their affluence simply because they believe the pastor would be clueless and have nothing to offer. When asked to clarify this position toward their pastors, they frequently replied that they would never turn to a clergyperson to find out how they should invest or manage a portfolio. They explained that they do not expect their pastor to have a clue about business and financial matters, mostly because the pastor has priorities of caring for the sick, the bereaved, and the teaching or preaching ministry. They do not see a connection of how the pastor could be helpful to them in matters of wealth.

This is an interesting observation when reversed; in other words, most pastors are frequently sought out for advice in the context of poverty. Furthermore, our research discovered that most pastors want no part in giving financial advice, as in investment strategies and the like.

Noteworthy is the fact that most people who are affluent do not consider themselves to be wealthy or affluent. Perhaps a bit more blessed than others, but really not affluent. Yet in the example above, the estate at stake might easily be worth $15 million if sold to a developer. Mom and dad might not consider themselves to be affluent. They have no investments and only a reasonable amount of cash reserves in their local bank savings account and CDs. If the estate, however, was liquidated and the proceeds from the sale divided equally among each child, each of those subsequent family's assets would have a sudden addition to their personal portfolios that exceeded three million dollars apiece. That would place them automatically not in the one percent but the top one-quarter of a percent of all American families. Translated, this means that 99.75 percent of the American population is below this net worth.

Here is a common situation that is evident in most families, namely, that there are millions of dollars being processed and transferred within the typical church membership, even if it is only 100 members in a rural congregation, a megachurch on the beltway, or a church that cares for some of the poorest communities. Money is changing hands. Wealth is being transferred. Values spiritual and tangible are being tested in these transactions.

Meanwhile the preacher preaches on about doctrines, topics, and scripture that stay above this fray, and delivers pastoral care as though no undercurrents are present—mostly because the laity keeps these issues out of the realm of the pastor's ear or concern, even while they stay awake at night agonizing over decisions that will affect members of their families, the church body, and the community at large.

So, what can the affluent yet spiritual person do to bring the gifts of ministry from the pastor to play in these real life issues? First, I suggest that the affluent member offer to equip the pastor by teaching him or her examples of points of stress. Second, they can pull back the veil that hides the underbelly of what is happening in the business world locally, in the family, and in the community—not as a point of gossip about the stress of others, not for investment advice, but as a point of connection with their personal issues around their affluence, the issues that come naturally to blessings and good fortune.

The clergy can take some initiative, as well, to bridge this gap. First, you can begin by asking to be taught. Seminary does not prepare a future clergyperson to know anything about business or finances. A healthy dose of curiosity is always helpful in the pastorate. This is different than nosiness. Curiosity conveys the sense of perpetual learning, equipping oneself to be aware of the context of those receiving the ministry. Asking permission to learn from parishioners is a good first step. Remain the student. Class is never over, regardless of the degrees you have earned.

Finally, in preparations for sermons, teaching sessions, and pastoral care visits, consider the perspective from the pew, the sickbed, the back-room office of a small business, or the executive suite of a corporation. What would you be thinking on that Sunday sitting in that pew with the crises of the past week or the critical decisions and actions that are on your agenda Monday morning?

REPRISE:

SUDDEN WEALTH

PASTOR TOM TAKES A bite of pound cake and another sip of coffee, buying time to think of how he will respond. He ponders for a second if he should take another bite of pound cake. Falling back on his natural pastoral skills, he replies, "Margaret, I sense that you are completely surprised by these two events. Is that correct?"

"Oh, Pastor Tom, I am in complete shock! Richard and I would talk occasionally about our finances. We always were careful about our debt. I trusted him to pay the bills, and we always talked before we made any kind of purchase like a car or something. He was never one to talk about death, or one of us having to live without the other. He always said I would be taken care of, and I just trusted that. I did not know how it would come about but figured he had everything planned out.

"We had been planning on retirement, having everything paid off when we reached the maximum age for Social Security for each of us. We only had three more years to go on our thirty-year mortgage on this house. He just put a new roof on it last year. The cars are paid for. He wanted to retire this year but decided we needed him to work three more years until we were both eligible for Medicare. Since he passed, I have been concerned about how to pay for healthcare coverage for the next two years."

Margaret's gaze drifted through the kitchen window to a spot somewhere on the back lawn when her voice went soft and then quiet.

"Margaret, Richard might not have talked much about taking care of you, but he took some serious actions some time ago to make these resources available to you today. What are some of your thoughts now that you have received these checks?"

"My thoughts are all over the place. Since that delivery yesterday, my stomach has been in a knot. Sounds crazy, doesn't it? One day I am worrying about how to buy health insurance until I get Medicare, and the next day I have all this!

"I didn't sleep a wink all night. A thousand things were rolling around in my head. I thought I was settling down and starting to move toward a normal routine the best I can. I am glad my oldest son took care of the funeral details and the cost of the service and burial. Thank you again for the wonderful job you did. The gravestone arrived last week and it looks wonderful. Hard to see it, but it helped put a closure to part of it. My stone is right next to it, with my date to be added." She pauses for a moment, and Tom sees that she is preparing to go on, perhaps into some deeper thoughts that she wants to share, so he just waits.

"After about a week, the regular bills started coming in. I didn't know what to do. I had my own checkbook, but he took care of all the monthly bills. I had a tax bill from the county. Stuff just kept coming, and I felt like I was drowning. A friend of mine recommended Joy Gilstrap. She provides a service to help widows and widowers organize all the bills and mail and paper stuff that just overwhelmed me. She came over immediately and worked miracles. Helped me get up to speed on whom to pay and when. As the bills from the hospital, the ambulance service, the doctors, and the insurance company started flowing, she helped me get that organized. God, I never knew so many people had seen him in his last hour. I couldn't have managed getting through it without someone like her.

"Richard always did our taxes. He liked the challenge even though he groused for a month getting all the stuff together and filing it. Joy put me in touch with an enrolled agent, Bill, who quickly took that burden off my mind.

"You would think that with two checks like these I would be dancing, figuring out where I could travel. Maybe throwing a big party. A part of me wants to do that. But the other part of me starts thinking about all the things around me. Should I pay off the mortgage? We have enough in savings that I could do that, but I'd have very little in reserve. Someone recommended Bobby, an estate attorney, who helped me begin probating the will. Glad we had that. But now I don't know how that fits into all this insurance money.

"I find it very lonely here at night, so my sister suggested having her 18-year-old daughter come live with me while she attends the community college here. But she has a boyfriend that looks to be no good to me, and he is always hanging around."

Tom listens, as Margaret's thoughts spill out like windblown tumbleweeds, disconnected, random. He lets each spin out its energy before being bumped by the next.

"Pastor Tom, what do you think I should do? I want to do the right thing."

Before he can respond, another tumbleweed spills out.

"I never dreamed I would have this much money. I had had my silly dreams about what I would do with winning the lottery. Give a lot of it away; make my friends and family happy with gifts I have always wanted to give; travel around the world; give the church a big gift; drive a new car every year . . . but this is different.

"Last night I could think of thousands of ways to use this money. My oldest boy, Ricky, is okay. He earns a good living. But I could help him with Trey's college. Maybe he would go to college if someone paid his way.

"And my other son—you remember Leslie—he's out of work, has been for over a year. His wife needs a hysterectomy, and they don't have any health insurance. They are about to lose their house.

"Speaking of houses, earlier this week I had the third offer to buy this house. Some folks are telling me to sell this place and move on. I am not so sure, but I do know that it is hard to keep up this yard. We had trouble with the oil heater last winter and I might have to replace it.

"Pastor Tom, you know very little about me, mostly because I keep everything to myself. I am a very private person. But I don't know where to turn."

There is a lengthy pause long enough to clue Tom in to the realization that Margaret is now ready for some kind of response. For the moment she is empty, but only for the moment.

Tom places a finger on the checks and looking up says gently, "Margaret, Richard took great care . . . to take good care of you . . . after he could not. Long ago he did all of this with you in mind. It seems to me that he did all of this so that you were provided with the resources you would need to live without him. You were primary in his thoughts.

"I understand your sense of shock. And I also appreciate your sense of being overwhelmed. There are indeed a lot of things to work through. They will require careful thought in order to make the best decisions for you. This unexpected boon in a time of grief should be a source of blessing for you.

"I sense that there are two things at work here. One is to discover how best to use these new resources in a way that will help you not just today and next week, but for the rest of your life. This is what financial advisors do, and I think you need one—someone you can trust, who will hear all your concerns, and will work with you to come up with a plan that you understand and will work for you, your goals.

"The other thing at work here is the practice of your faith in a new setting that is unfamiliar to you. You might say that by most standards, you are now a very wealthy lady. And now you have new resources you must manage. I believe that your faith will guide you to make the best decisions for yourself as Richard intended and then to go on to make any additional decisions. I will be at your side to help you through those times and you can call on me anytime you want to discuss such matters.

"Yes, I've noticed that you are very private person. And keeping these concerns private while you search for the right solutions is very important to you. I thank you for your confidence in me as you have shared your burden with me today. I want to assure you I will honor your confidence and privacy.

"I suggested that a financial advisor might assist you to help you process much of what is overwhelming you in this new experience. I would further suggest that you use the help of someone who is competent, who listens to you, and who will work with you to find the best solutions, someone that has your best interest at heart. Do you have someone in mind that you can turn to?"

"Pastor, I wouldn't have the first clue of where to turn. That's part of the reason I called you today. I know your expertise is not financial stuff, but all of this money has suddenly made me a bit uncomfortable. I don't know what to do, but I want to do what is right. What do you suggest?"

"You are right, Margaret. My strongest suit is teaching and preaching. But you are also right in seeing how events like today push our faith into areas beyond our usual comfort zone. I want to work with you on this.

"As your pastor, I am deeply concerned about your welfare. You know I consider you one of my sheep and I don't want you falling victim to wolves. I have seen many cases where relatives, friends—even strangers—come out of the woodwork in attempts to get their hands on someone's good fortune. I do not want that to happen to you. So, I am suggesting that you take a few simple steps to get some professional help. I suggest you not cash these checks until after you have spoken with an attorney who specializes in estate planning. I can help you find one if you need me to. That attorney might suggest a trust account or some other legal instrument to protect these resources while you make some important decisions.

"Second, I recommend you find a good financial advisor. You might want to shop around for one that suits you. I know a few financial advisors. Some are members of our church, and some are completely outside of this community. I will be glad to provide you with their contact information.

"Along those lines, I want give you permission to exercise a bit of freedom on this matter. Choosing your financial advisor should be a good fit for you. You should feel very comfortable. You should not feel intimidated in your discussions. So I recommend you check out at least two and perhaps more. Listen to your feelings and your gut to guide you in making that choice."

Tom pauses and lets Margaret absorb these suggestions. As she picks up the conversation again, he senses that she is much less tense. She is beginning to discuss her other concerns in an orderly fashion much as she has always done, even in the early stages of her grief. A few minutes later and another cup of coffee with another slice of pound cake, Tom begins sending all the usual signals that he must leave for other appointments, including an offer to pray, asking, "Margaret, we have addressed some very important and new things in your life today. As we pray, is there anything specific you would like me to include in our prayer for you?"

She mentions a desire for a sense of peace, guidance, and healing. Tom then offers a gracious, simple prayer of gratitude for Richard's kindness and thoughtfulness many years ago and for the ongoing grace of God that sustains and guides us in times of grief, in times of need, and in times of blessings.

For Further Reading

Atkinson, Steven, Joni Clark, Eric Goldberg, and Alex Potts. (2011). *The Wealth Solution, Bringing Structure to Your Financial Life*, with foreword by Mark G. Cooke, J. Robert Moon, and David Morton. San Jose, CA: Loring Ward, copies available by request.

Killinger, John. (2012). *The Zacchaeus Solution: How Christians Can Reverse the World's Economic Downturn*. Warrenton, VA: The Intermundia Press.

Moon, Robert and Mark Cooke. (2011). *Pastoral Care in the Context of Sudden Wealth—Research on How Clergy Are or Are Not Engaging in Life-Changing Wealth Events*. A white paper available by email request to jrobertmoon@gmail.com

EARLY ON MY FATHER taught me that stewardship is more than subscribing to a church budget. Stewardship, he said, is the practice of using what you have to better another's station in life. As a pastor for nearly fifty years it seemed that I spent most of my time during financial emphasis seasons talking about raising money, meeting the budget, paying the bills; little of importance was ever said about true stewardship. . . . Like most pastors, I settled for immediate results rather than helping the wealthy understand how to use their wealth for global purposes. Bob Moon has demonstrated in his book, My Pastor, My Money, and Why We're Not Talking *where I short-changed those who had wealth. Private conversations with those persons would have been welcomed. . . .*

I encourage young pastors to read this little book, apply its principles to their ministry, and seek out a trusted financial advisor who can help them understand how wealth can be a blessing, not a curse. Today there are many more persons of wealth . . . ready for their pastor to help them be good stewards of their blessings. They know that a poverty of spirit in matters of wealth means a poverty of spirit in all things. Bob Moon's advice makes for a healthy life-style for pastor and laity.

— Rev. Dr. Dallas Stallings
Durham, North Carolina

*M*R. MOON WRITES WELL. . . . *I felt as if I were speaking with him, as a matter of fact. Mr. Moon is dead on, reminding the reader that stewardship is more than just money (treasure).*

— Father Victor Ulto, Pastor
St. Bernadette Catholic Church
Port St. Lucie, Florida

*B*OB DOES A GOOD JOB OF *exploring what is usually a taboo sub-ject in churches—dealing with personal wealth, especially when it is newly acquired. He gives helpful, realistic examples to address the myth that increase in wealth is an unmitigated blessing and to challenge the assumption that such a "blessing" is by definition tainted. I especially like the way in which he portrays pastoral care in terms of listening well and naming the concerns of the parishioner, but not needing to hold the expertise. I suspect that many pastors avoid discussing financial concerns because of their own lack of fi-nancial knowledge. His clear, straightforward writing evidences com-passion for pastors and laypeople as they attempt to respond faithfully to the challenges of wealth.*

— Dr. Kathleen W. Kurtz, LPC
Manassas, Virginia

*I*AM GUILTY OF HAVING *A degree of bias towards extraordinarily rich people—not all of them, of course, because I have been the beneficiary on occasion of their generosity. I appreciate your struggle to help people like me with this issue as you help yourself. I find your* *insight to be practical and helpful and it prompts me to reasses my bias.*

— Jim Strickland, Co-director
The Sabbath House
Bryson City, North Carolina

*E*VERY ONCE IN A WHILE *a book appears addressing a subject that no other book has addressed, but one for which there is a real need. I know of no author that zeros in on the issue of pastoral care of wealthy persons in a congregation like Bob Moon does in* My Pastor, My Money, and Why We're Not Talking, *which effectively bridges the gap between pastors and those with wealth. Coming at this neglected subject with dual experience and credentials in both pastoral ministry and financial advising, Bob Moon helps pastors understand the various ways people gain large wealth and the attitudes that can accompany that wealth. I highly recommend this helpful and engaging volume to pastoral caregivers who are seeking to increase their depth of awareness and repertoire of responses in regard to wealthy persons in their congregations, as well as to those wealthy members themselves.*

— C. Roy Woodruff, PhD, LPC
Diplomate and Retired Executive Director
American Association of Pastoral Counselors

*I*HAVE BEEN A PASTOR, *senior minister, and priest of at least eight congregations in my 51 years in ministry. Every one of them had* *persons of wealth. In at least two of my churches, there were a number of very wealthy people. Did I converse with them? Yes, but not in such depth or with such a focused purpose as Bob Moon suggests in his most excellent work,* My Pastor, My Money, and Why We're Not Talking. *It is my privilege in my psychotherapy and spiritual direction ministry to have worked with clergy from at least ten denominations and to counsel some in the process of Episcopal priesthood. I have a list of "must reads" for these persons, and now Bob Moon's book will be at the top of the list. I heartily recommend this work without reservation for every pastor, priest, and minister who wants to relate effectively to persons of wealth.*

— The Reverend Canon Thomas H. Conley, ThM
Former senior minister of the Northside Drive Baptist Church; retired canon pastor of the Episcopal Cathedral of St. Philip; and founder, psychotherapist, and executive director emeritus, the Conley Center for Care, Counseling, and Psychotherapy, all in Atlanta, Georgia

*B*OB MOON'S TIMELY BOOK *is filled with practical insights in helping clergy and laity speak openly and honestly about a topic few have dared to broach with the care that is needed. Concise and engaging, readers will feel empowered to share and respond in new ways to "bridge the gap" that too often exists between those with wealth and the pastors who seek to care for them.*

— Rudy Tucker, Senior Pastor
Grace United Methodist Church Manassas, Virginia

I THINK YOU ARE REALLY ON to something with the whole insight into the lack of pastoral care for the wealthy and the issues of sudden wealth.

— Don Meeks, Senior Pastor
Greenwich Presbyterian Church
Nokesville, Virginia

CPSIA information can be obtained at www.ICGtesting.com
Printed in the USA
BVOW071512251112

306216BV00001B/35/P